A Plastic Toy

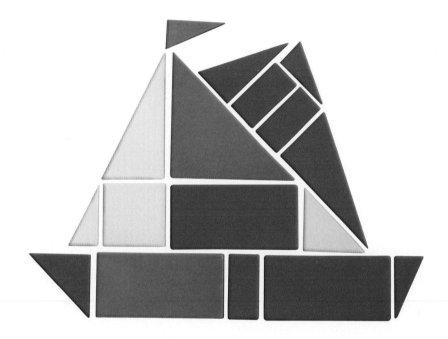

Sue Barraclough

GARETH**STEVENS**
GS
PUBLISHING
A Member of the WRC Media Family of Companies

The author and publishers would like to thank Invicta Plastics and Hampton Colours for their help with this book.

Please visit our web site at: www.garethstevens.com
For a free color catalog describing Gareth Stevens Publishing's list of high-quality books
and multimedia programs, call 1·800·542·2595 (USA) or 1·800·387·3178 (Canada).
Gareth Stevens Publishing's fax: (414) 332·3567.

Library of Congress Cataloging·in·Publication Data

Barraclough, Sue.
  A plastic toy / Sue Barraclough.
    p. cm. — (How it's made)
  ISBN·10: 0-8368-6704-1 — ISBN·13: 978-0-8368-6704-6 (lib. bdg.)
  1. Plastics—Juvenile literature. 2. Plastic toys—Juvenile literature. I. Title. II. Series.
TP1089.B37   2006
668.4—dc22   2006042298

This North American edition first published in 2007 by
Gareth Stevens Publishing
A Member of the WRC Media Family of Companies
330 West Olive Street, Suite 100
Milwaukee, WI 53212 USA

This U.S. edition copyright © 2007 by Gareth Stevens, Inc.
Original edition copyright © 2006 by Franklin Watts.
First published in Great Britain in 2006 by Franklin Watts,
338 Euston Road, London NW1 3BH, United Kingdom.

Series editor: Sarah Peutrill
Art director: Jonathan Hair
Designer: Jemima Lumley

Gareth Stevens editor: Tea Benduhn
Gareth Stevens art direction: Tammy West
Gareth Stevens graphic designer: Charlie Dahl

Photo credits: (t=top, b=bottom, l=left, r=right, c=center)
Ancient Art & Architecture Collection/Topfoto: 5b. CORBIS: 8, 26bl. Townsed P. Dickinson/Image Works/Topfoto: 3lt.
Digital Vision: 9b. Franklin Watts: 19t, 28, 29t. Lowell Georgia/CORBIS: 4b, 26tl. Courtesy of Hampton Colours: 1ltr, 1lc.
Courtesy of Invicta Plastics: 1lb, 12t, 13bl. Cindy Lewis Car Photos/Alamy: 17b. Richard Lord/Image Works/Topfoto: 6b.
Maximillian Stock/Science Photo Library: 9t. Jackson Smith/Alamy: 29b. Paul A. Souders/CORBIS: 7t. Syracuse Newspapers/
Li·Hua Lan/Image Works/Topfoto: 3lb. Topfoto: 6t, 26cl, 30b. Roger Wood/CORBIS: 7b. All other photography by Andy
Crawford/Franklin Watts. Every effort has been made to trace the copyright holders for the photos used in this book.
The publisher apologizes, in advance, for any unintentional omissions and would be pleased to insert the appropriate
acknowledgements in any subsequent edition of this publication.

Printed in the United States of America

1 2 3 4 5 6 7 8 9 10 09 08 07 06

Words that appear in the glossary are printed in
boldface type the first time they occur in the text.

Contents

These toy shapes are made of plastic 4

Crude oil is found deep under the ground 6

Crude oil is treated and processed at an oil refinery 8

The chemicals are made into plastic granules 10

Designers plan and create the toy shapes 12

A mold for the shapes is designed and built 14

Plastic granules are sent to the toy factory 16

An injection molding machine is prepared 18

Plastic granules are fed into the molding machine 20

The pieces are cooled and pushed out of the mold 22

The finished toy shapes are sorted and packed 24

How a Plastic Toy Is Made 26

Plastic and Its Many Uses 28

Plastic and the Environment 30

Glossary/Index 32

These toy shapes are made of plastic.

The story of a plastic toy starts with a substance called crude oil. **Chemicals** are taken from crude oil to make most kinds of plastic. The chemicals are **processed** into different types of plastic.

These colored pieces of plastic can be used to create patterns and pictures.

Plastics often have long names. The colored shapes pictured in this book are made out of a plastic called polypropylene copolymer.

Crude oil is usually black and thick. Some crude oil is runny and clear, but most of it looks like dark syrup.

4

Why plastic?

Plastic is a popular material to use because it can be made into objects quickly and easily. It can be **molded** to make different shapes such as bottles and pipes. It can be pressed and stretched into flat sheets. It can be made into fibers that can be woven to make clothes. Plastic can be hard and clear like glass, soft and thick like a sponge, or thin and flexible like paper.

The word plastic comes from the Greek word *plastikos*, which means something that can be shaped and molded.

Plastics are popular materials for making toys because they are tough and waterproof, and they can be brightly colored.

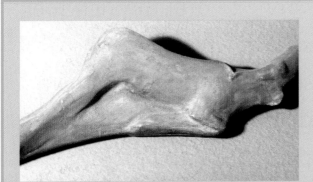

This prehistoric bone carving shows an early use of shaping a natural material.

In the Past

Early humans discovered that materials such as bone, horn, and rubbery gums from tropical trees could be made into objects. Over time, people learned to melt, mold, and shape these materials. Later, scientists created **synthetic** plastics out of natural materials.

Crude oil is found deep under the ground.

Crude oil is a natural substance that is usually found trapped between layers of rock deep under the ground. To reach crude oil, people need to use huge machines such as oil rigs with powerful drills.

Oil rigs can drill on land or in the ocean.

The drill heads must be very strong to drill through rock, so they are usually made of strong steel and superhard diamonds. A very long pipeline carries the crude oil back to an oil rig.

Oil crews operate the huge machinery.

Some oil tankers are so big that the crews use bicycles to travel from one end to the other.

Huge amounts of crude oil are pumped out of the ground every day. The oil is taken to oil **refineries** to be processed. Sometimes large ships called tankers transport the oil by sea.

Sometimes the oil is pumped through pipelines that stretch across land.

What is crude oil?

Crude oil formed over millions of years from the remains of plants and animals. It is often found very deep under the ground in pockets that are under layers of rock. Most crude oil is made into **fuels** that can be used for heating and transportation. There is a limited amount of crude oil in the earth. One day it will run out.

This pipeline takes oil to a refinery.

Crude oil is treated and processed at an oil refinery.

Crude oil has to be changed, or processed, before it is useful. At the oil refinery, it is broken down into useful parts such as fuels, other gases, and chemicals. The chemicals can be used to make plastics.

Oil refineries have docks where tankers unload crude oil. They have pipelines, containers, and machines to refine the crude oil.

This scientist is testing a liquid plastic to see how quickly it hardens as it cools.

To create plastics, chemicals are heated and broken down into very small parts called monomers. These monomers are the basic building blocks used to make different plastics. They can be made into products such as very strong car bumpers, thin plastic bags, and even fabrics for clothes.

In the Past

In 1951, two chemists named J. Paul Hogan and Robert L. Banks were trying to make a type of fuel. When a sticky, white substance clogged their equipment, they realized the substance could be useful. They carefully recorded the way they made the substance so they could recreate it. Their discovery led to the **manufacture** of polypropylene, which is a type of plastic.

Most crude oil is made into fuels such as gasoline.

The chemicals are made into plastic granules.

The plastic shapes pictured on the cover of this book are made using two types of plastic granules. One type of granule is colorless and almost see-through. Colorless granules are the main ingredient in these toy shapes.

Colorless granules can look white when many of them are together.

There are three types of masterbatch granules used to make the three colors of the plastic toy shapes — red, blue, and yellow.

The other type of granule is called masterbatch, which is a special ingredient used to make each type of plastic. Just a tiny amount of masterbatch adds color to the finished plastics.

Colorless and masterbatch granules are both made at a plastic factory. To make the granules, first the chemical substance is heated to make it soft. Then it is squeezed through a machine that forms it into long strands.

The yellow masterbatch is squeezed into strands.

The yellow masterbatch is now in granules.

When the strands cool, they harden. The hard strands are chopped into small pieces called granules.

The toy makers choose the color of masterbatch granules they want.

The toy makers use samples to check the color of plastic the granules will make.

Designers plan and create the toy shapes.

Before the plastic granules can be used, the toy company must **design** the toy shapes.

Computer Aided Design (CAD) helps designers make plans.

First, designers discuss and sketch ideas. Then they decide every detail of the design including the size, shape, color, and type of plastic.

Even a very simple plastic product needs to be planned and designed carefully.

Once a design is finalized, a **prototype**, or a model, is made. The model might be made in different colors or with different plastics to test out the options and to see what looks and works best.

Testing Plastic Toys

Toys must be tested carefully to make sure they are safe to use. The manufacturer has to be sure the toy will not be able to choke a child, that it is not toxic or poisonous, and that it has no sharp edges. Toys are also tested with children to make sure they are useful and fun.

Light

In the sharp test, a special tool that looks like a pen is used to touch the plastic. If the tool lights up, the toy is too sharp.

The plastic company tests their products in a school to make sure they work properly.

In the choke test, pieces are put in a small tube. If they fit in the tube, the pieces are too small.

A mold for the shapes is designed and built.

When the final toy design is decided, a mold will be made to shape the plastic. The mold needs to be built very carefully. After it is completed, it will be used to make many of the same plastic pieces.

Molds are designed using a computer.

A designer draws and checks the plans for the mold.

When the mold design is ready, a machine makes a steel mold for the plastic toy shapes. Steel is used because it is a metal that will not bend or break easily, and it lasts a long time.

A computer controls the mold machine. The machine uses drills to make the parts of the mold.

The block of steel is very heavy!

Steel or aluminum?

If a mold will be used to make fewer than ten thousand pieces, it is made of aluminum. A mold is made of long-lasting, strong steel if it will make more than ten thousand pieces. The toy shapes pictured in this book have been made in large numbers for more than thirty years, so the mold is made from a steel block.

Plastic granules are sent to the toy factory.

After a mold is built, it is ready to make plastic toy shapes. Meanwhile, boxes of plastic granules are loaded on a truck and sent to the toy factory.

Boxes of granules are placed on a truck.

The granules are stacked in a **warehouse** until they are ready to be used. Both colorless granules and masterbatch in red, yellow, and blue are needed to make the toy shapes.

Colorless granules are stacked in bags.

After the plastic granules have arrived, the mold is taken to the machine that will make the plastic toy.

The mold is very heavy, so it is wheeled into the factory on a trolley.

Why plastic?

Plastic is a strong, lightweight material. It can be made into a wide range of different products from cling wrap that is light and flexible to window frames that are hard and strong.

Many parts of cars are now made of plastic because it can be light but very strong.

An injection molding machine is prepared.

The injection molding machine has several parts.

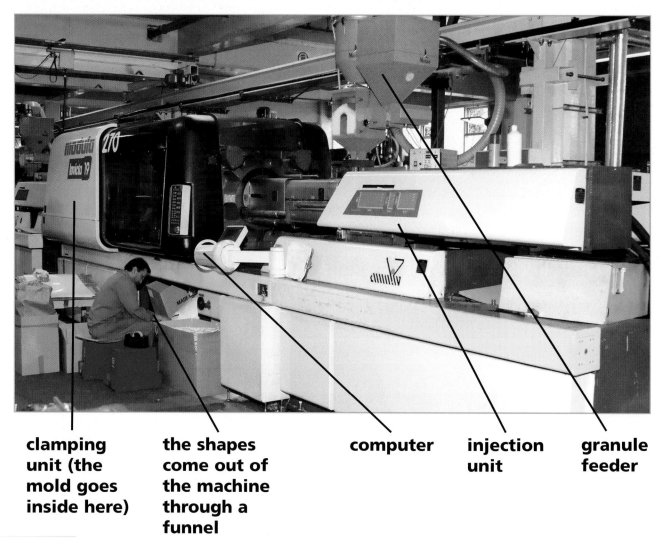

clamping unit (the mold goes inside here) **the shapes come out of the machine through a funnel** **computer** **injection unit** **granule feeder**

An injection molding machine is used to make the toy shapes. The machine can make many pieces at one time.

The mold for the plastic toy shapes is placed inside the machine. After the mold is in place, a computer controls the injection molding machine.

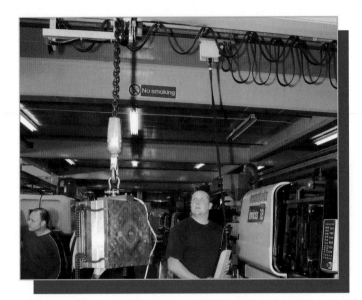

A small crane lifts the mold into the machine.

The machine's computer needs to be programmed, or "told what to do." A worker types in information about the running time and temperature.

Molding Machines

Different types of molding machines use different ways to push plastic into a mold. The injection molding machine squirts liquid plastic into a mold. Other machines push, blow, or squeeze plastic to fill a mold to make the right shape.

Bottles are made with a blow mold. Air is blown into the plastic to push it to the sides of a mold. This process makes a hollow plastic shape.

Plastic granules are fed into the molding machine.

The plastic toy shapes are made of 99 percent colorless granules and 1 percent masterbatch.

A large supply of colorless granules is kept in a hopper.

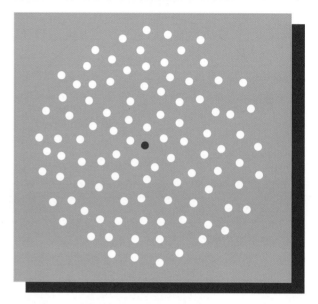

Only a tiny amount of masterbatch is needed.

The colorless granules are placed in a container called a hopper. The hopper is linked to the injection molding machine by a pipe that runs across the factory's ceiling.

pipe to molding machine

granules

hopper

The small amount of masterbatch granules are fed directly into the machine. Yellow masterbatch is used to make yellow toy shapes.

Two types of granules are in feeders that are attached to the machine.

colorless granules   **yellow masterbatch**

sprue

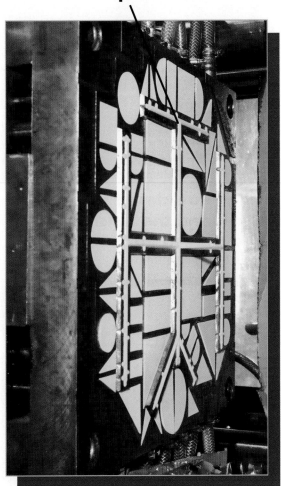

Colorless and masterbatch plastic granules are heated to 392 °Fahrenheit (200 °Celsius). The granules melt to become a very hot liquid which is then forced into the mold. The machine applies pressure to the liquid to make sure the mold is completely filled with plastic.

One mold can make sixty-two toy shapes at one time. The toy shapes are attached to a branch-like piece of plastic, called a sprue, that connects the pieces to each other inside the mold.

The pieces are cooled and pushed out of the mold.

When the pieces are cool, the mold opens. The machine cuts the toy shapes away from the sprue and pushes them out of the mold. The pieces fall into a funnel. At the other end of the funnel, workers collect the pieces.

A funnel makes it easier to catch the shapes in a bag.

The two sides of the mold open and the finished pieces are pushed out.

Old sprues are collected in a box. They will then be ground up and reused as plastic granules.

The discarded sprue will be reused.

The machine will make hundreds of batches of yellow pieces. When the machine has made enough yellow pieces, it is heated to a very high temperature to clean away any leftover plastic. Then a new masterbatch color is added to the colorless granules and put into the mold. The machine makes the same number of toy shape pieces in blue and then red.

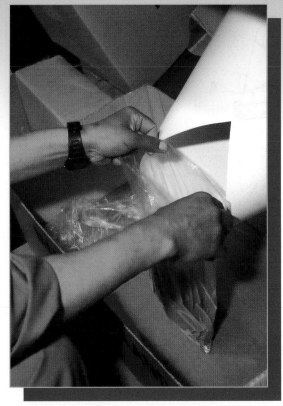

The machine makes a batch of blue shapes next.

Plastic Symbols

There are many types of plastic, and each one is made with a different mixture of chemicals. A symbol is printed on a plastic object to show what type of plastic it is. Before plastics can be **recycled**, they need to be sorted into types.

This is the symbol for polypropylene.

5 PP

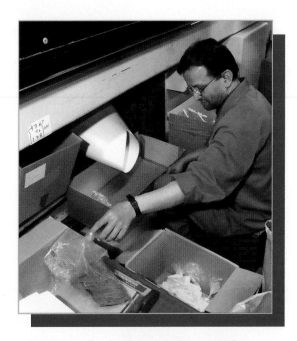

Then red shapes are made to complete the set. Here a worker weighs them.

The finished toy shapes are sorted and packed.

The toy shapes are put into bags that are also made of plastic.

In the packing room, workers put a bag of each toy shape color into a larger bag. Then they put the packages of toy shapes into boxes. They seal and label the boxes and store them in a warehouse.

Boxes are packed carefully so they can be transported safely.

The plastic toy shapes are ready to send to shops and schools. People can then make pictures with the toy shapes.

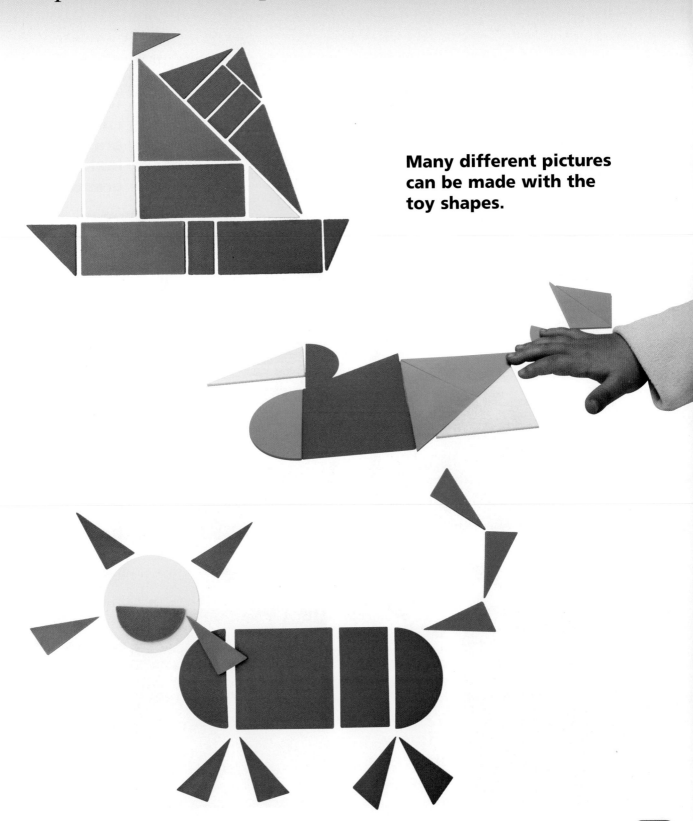

Many different pictures can be made with the toy shapes.

How a Plastic Toy Is Made

 **1. Most plastics are made from crude oil.**

 **4. Chemicals taken from crude oil are used to make plastic granules.**

2. Crude oil is drilled from under the ground.

 **5. Toy designers plan the toy shapes and their mold.**

 **3. An oil refinery processes the crude oil.**

 **6. The mold is brought to the machine.**

10. The finished pieces are pushed out and caught in a bag.

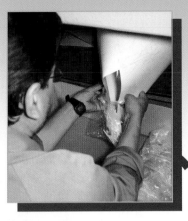

11. Workers sort the toy shapes and put them into bags.

9. Hot plastic cools in the mold.

12. Bags of toy shapes are put into boxes which are taped up and ready to be shipped.

8. Color masterbatch granules are added to the mix.

13. The toy shapes are used to create patterns and pictures.

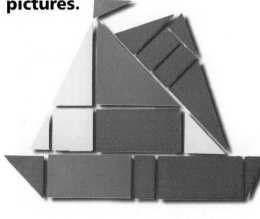

7. Colorless granules are put into a hopper, which feeds them into the machine.

Plastic and Its Many Uses

Plastic is used to make many different products, from toys to car parts. It has replaced other packaging materials because plastic is sturdier than paper or cardboard, and it is stronger and much lighter than glass.

Plastic bags are light but strong, so they are ideal for carrying groceries.

Fruit and vegetables are put in plastic containers and covered with plastic film to protect them and keep them clean.

Polystyrene is a type of plastic material that is mixed with air to make it soft and light. It is often used for packaging.

Before plastic was invented, combs were made of materials such as bone or wood.

Plastic bottles are light and easy to carry around, and they will not break if they are dropped. Plastic lunch boxes keep food clean and dry.

This flashlight is made with strong plastic. The waterproof casing keeps the batteries and lightbulb dry.

Sunglasses are made from two different types of plastic — one for the frame and one that protects eyes from the sun.

Fleece fabric is very warm.

From Plastic Bottles to Fluffy Fleece

Did you know that a certain type of plastic can be recycled to make fleece fabric? The plastic is Polyethylene Terephthalate (PET), which is often used to make bottles for soft drinks. First, the labels and bottle caps are removed. Then the bottles are chopped into plastic flakes. The flakes are heated and melted, and the soft plastic is pushed through holes in a machine, which makes them into long strands. The strands are stretched and squeezed and then fluffed and cooled. This process makes fibers that can be woven into fleece fabric.

Plastic and the Environment

While many plastic products are made to be used again and again, most plastic packaging is made to be thrown away. The main problem with plastic waste is that it does not biodegrade, which means that it does not break down or rot.

Lightweight Plastics

Plastics are ideal for packaging because they can be very lightweight.

Plastic packaging protects food and keeps it clean and fresh, which cuts down on food waste.

These lightweight plastics can be blown by the wind very easily. Plastic trash in our environment does not look nice, and it can be dangerous if it gets caught in streams or drains.

Plastic litter can be blown out of trash bags and cans, and it can get caught in trees and bushes.

Plastic and Wildlife

Plastic waste and litter can be dangerous for wildlife. Gulls search piles of trash for food, and they can swallow plastic waste or get it caught on their legs or heads. Sea turtles swallow and choke on plastic bags, which they mistake for jellyfish, their favorite food.

A bird is caught in a piece of plastic waste.

Before plastic can be recycled by machines, people usually have to sort it by hand into different types.

Recycling Plastics

Recycling plastic saves energy, and it cuts down on pollution. Recycling can be difficult because there are so many types of plastic. Each type needs to be recycled separately. In order for recycling to be worth the effort, people need to recycle more used plastic, and they need to make sure the plastic they buy is made from recycled plastic.

Glossary

chemicals – the individual substances that mix together to make up other substances, either natural or manufactured

design – to plan something that will be made, by making drawings, choosing materials, and deciding on shapes, colors, and patterns

fuels – substances that are burned to make heat or power

manufacture – the process of making a product, especially on a large scale, using machinery

molded – shaped. Objects can be shaped by pressing plastic or other materials into a special container called a mold.

processed – caused a change by using a series of actions

prototype – a model that is made to test materials, patterns, and colors

recycled – made into useful material from material that has already been used

refineries – factories that separate mixtures into their different parts

sprue – [pronounced SPROO] a branch-shaped piece of plastic that is formed in a mold and connects pieces of useful plastic to each other

synthetic – a material made in a factory using chemicals

temperature – a measure of heat

warehouse – a building where things are stored

Index

chemicals 4, 8, 9, 10, 11, 23, 26
computers 12, 14, 15, 18, 19
crude oil 4, 6, 7, 8, 9, 26

fabrics 9, 29
fuel 7, 8, 9

molding machine 18, 19, 20

oil refinery 8, 26

packaging 24, 28, 30
pipelines 6, 7, 8
plastic,
    granules 10, 11, 12, 16, 17, 18, 20, 21, 22, 23, 26, 27
    hard 5, 9, 11, 17
    masterbatch 10, 11, 16, 20, 21, 23, 27

recycling 23, 29, 31
scientists 5, 9
sprue 21, 22
toy,
    design 12, 13, 14, 15, 26
    molds 14, 15, 16, 17, 18, 19, 21, 22, 23, 26, 27
    testing 13